VIRTUALLY WORKING

LEGAL NOTICE

While all attempts have been made to verify information provided in this publication, the Publisher assumes no responsibility for errors, omissions, or contrary interpretation of the subject matter herein. Any perceived slights of specific persons, peoples, or organizations are unintentional.

In practical advice books, like anything else in life, there are no guarantees of income made. Readers are cautioned to reply on their own judgment about their individual circumstances to act accordingly.

This book is not intended for use as a source of legal, business, accounting, or financial advice. All readers are advised to seek services of competent professionals in the legal, business, accounting, and finance fields.

Daniel Holliday

VIRTUALLY WORKING

HOW TO PURCHASE YOUR FIRST VACATION RENTAL

Overland Park, KS
www.vacationincome.info
holliday@vacationincome.info

SCAN THIS CODE
and search for Florida Vacation Rentals

Virtually Working
Copyright ©2020. Daniel Holliday
Published by Freeman Holdings LLC
Overland Park, KS
www.vacationincome.info
holliday@vacationincome.info

ISBN 978-1-7352630-2-1 (ebook)
ISBN 978-1-7352630-3-8 (paperback)

All rights reserved. No portion of this book may be copied, reproduced or transmitted in any form without written permission from the publisher.

Printed in the United States of America

Table of Contents

INTRODUCTION — i.

CHAPTER 1 - Location, Location, Location — 1

CHAPTER 2 - Working with Real Estate Agents — 13

CHAPTER 3 - Watching the Housing Market — 31

CHAPTER 4 - Home Inspections — 45

CHAPTER 5 - Financing Your Vacation or Second Home — 65

CHAPTER 6 - Making a Realistic Offer — 89

CHAPTER 7 - Contracts, Home Warranties, and Closing — 107

CONCLUSION — 115

Introduction

If you currently live in an apartment, rent a house, or own a home you may be thinking about buying a vacation home of your own for yourself and your family. This can be an exciting time but it can also be daunting depending on who you have working on your team. Looking at properties, deciding whether to buy a vacation home or build a new one, and finding financing will take up a lot of your time...but don't fret, it's doable.

There will be a long list of things you will need to do before you buy a vacation home. This list includes:

- Choosing a real estate agent
- Finding the right neighborhood
- Finding a vacation home that fits your needs
- Finding the features you desire
- Choosing the right size yard
- Understanding the housing market
- The ins and outs of vacation home inspections
- Reviewing contracts
- Financing
- Making an offer

This list does not include all the decorating, home improvements, and other decisions you should make once you have purchased the vacation home.

If you are a first-time home buyer, you will be nervous about finding the right vacation home, investing money on a down payment, and being approved for financing. Once you have found a vacation home, it will usually take up to 60 days before you will be able to move in. In the meantime, you should plan the following:

- Moving arrangements
- Yard sales
- Budgeting for paint and other supplies
- Taking time off from work
- Prepping the family
- Changing utilities

Proper planning will help you transition into ownership much easier than if you wait until the last minute to deal with these details.

New vs Older Vacation Homes

Another decision you should make is whether to buy a new vacation home or look for an older one. Most first time homebuyers usually buy an older home, but this should not deter you from having your agent help you find a few builders that are building in your price range.

Older vacation homes may cost less, but they can have more problems. In this book, you will learn what to look for when viewing a vacation home, what to include in your purchase offer, and what to expect during the inspection. There are many older vacation homes that will need only minor repairs so don't shut out those vacation homes.

Which Vacation Home to Choose?
After you have considered all your options, you will be wondering which vacation home to choose. There are many ways to find the vacation home that is right for you. When looking at vacation homes, you should keep these criteria in mind:

- Family needs
- Features
- Size
- Price
- Neighborhood/community
- Mortgage payments
- Repairs
- Condo association dues

While this is a short list, throughout this book you will learn other ways to find your dream vacation home. In the end, you will know when you have found the right vacation home!

Purchasing your first vacation home will be an experience you will never forget. You should be excited as this is where you will create a lot of memories with your family. Whether this is the home you will own for a few years or a few decades, buying a vacation home will give you a sense of pride and of purpose. When thinking about purchasing a vacation home, you should begin saving your money for closing costs, repairs, and decorating.

One of the more rewarding moments will be when you get the keys to your new vacation home and you begin making it your own with a little paint, furniture, and personal style.

Chapter 1

Choosing where to live and invest your money is almost as important as the type of home you want to purchase and live in. While this is a very personal decision, there are pros and cons to every neighborhood. But wherever you want to live and invest, you should know where the highways are located, grocery stores, schools, and how far from work and other amenities you will be. Buying a vacation home means more than the structure you will be living and investing in. It is also the community and the accessibility to places and events that mean the most to you, your family and vacationers.

Finding the Right Neighborhood

How will you know you have found the right neighborhood? There are many ways to tell:

- You may feel a sense of calm
- The neighborhood may remind you of a happy memory
- The neighborhood aesthetics are pleasing
- The rest of your family is pleased

You may feel one emotion or five when you turn the corner onto the street where you want to live. This will be an exciting time, especially if you have been searching for a vacation home for the past few months.

When looking for the right location, you should consider the following:

- How clean is this neighborhood?
- Are the schools nearby?
- Is this a high crime area?
- What is the average vacation home value in the neighborhood?
- Are there community bylaws?
- What is the vacation home close to?
- Is there garbage pickup?

While these questions may not include everything you are looking for when buying a vacation home, they should be considered carefully as they will affect your life once you move into the vacation home.

How Clean Is This Neighborhood?

You should look at the neighborhood at different times during the day to see how those who live in the neighborhood take care of it. If there is a lot of trash on the ground, the yards are not kept up properly, or there are old signs posted on trees and telephone poles, then the neighborhood may not be for you.

If the neighborhood looks clean and you see people outside caring for their lawns, then you may have found a community of people who care about where they live. All too often people will buy vacation homes only to discover that it is in a neighborhood where people do not have respect for their property or the property of others. This can make selling the vacation home much more difficult in the future.

Is This An Area Prone to Crime or Peddling?

While all neighborhoods will experience some crime, be careful when you consider buying a vacation home in an area that has a high crime rate. While the vacation home itself may be the right price for your budget, it may not be in an area that is right for your well-being.

Drive by the neighborhood at nighttime to see if there is adequate street lighting, suspicious activity, or anything else that might cause you to use caution. Research the neighborhood and find out how the crime rate compares to other neighborhoods. If the crime rate is too high, then it may be best to look somewhere else.

What Is the Average Home Value in The Neighborhood?

You can find this information out very easily by asking your agent or by looking up this information at the county clerk's office or on their web site. You should be aware of the vacation home values that are in your neighborhood for several reasons:

- Housing prices will vary depending on the neighborhood and region. You want to buy a vacation home that you will be able to make a profit on when you decide to sell.
- You do not want to pay too much for a vacation home.
- Giving a solid offer for the vacation home means knowing what other vacation homes that are similar in size are selling for.

Are There Community Bylaws?

If you are looking at a vacation home that is inside a community, you should be aware of yearly dues, what you can leave in your driveway and even how you decorate. So, pay close attention.

Many people enjoy living in a community because they feel safe and want to meet others in the neighborhood. Communities usually have picnics and other events during the year where neighbors can meet each other. Some communities have pools, tennis courts, game rooms and other amenities.

What Is the Vacation Home Close To?

When choosing a vacation home, you will need to find the nearest grocery store, schools, route to work, and other necessities that will make living in the neighborhood more convenient. Drive around the neighborhood to see what is around it. This will help make your decision to buy a vacation home in a neighborhood much easier.

Is There Garbage Pickup?

While this may not seem like something you are interested in, when it comes to disposing of your trash, you may need to haul it to the dump yourself. Ask about trash pickup so that you can decide if this is something you want to do or have a service do for you. Trash disposal is often covered in community bylaws for a monthly or quarterly fee.

City Life vs. Country Living vs. Suburbs vs. Beach Life

Choosing the community, you want to invest in will also include deciding whether you want your guests to enjoy the city, country, suburbs or beach. People with families usually want to live in the suburbs because there is more room for children to grow and play, but is still close enough for parents to commute to work. However those wouldn't be the same reasons why and where they choose to vacation.

There are advantages to the city and staying near the beach as well. Those who stay in the city will be close to restaurants, activities, and events. Those who invest in the country may have a longer commute to access amenities, but they will be able to enjoy the peace and quiet of having fewer people around them. Also if the lot or property is large enough you may consider using it as an event venue for hosting outdoor weddings or a bed & breakfast at a cabin in the mountains or woods.

Whichever lifestyle your guests prefer, you should construct a pros and cons list that will give you a better idea of what to expect when looking for a vacation home. Once you have looked at your list, you will have a better idea of which to choose. The following will get you started:

CITY LIFE

PROS
- Easy access to cultural events
- More options when eating out
- More grocery store and clothing store options
- Public transportation
- More people
- Choice of vacation home styles, such as traditional houses, condos, apartments

CONS
- Crime rates higher
- Pollution
- More people
- Higher housing costs
- Higher taxes
- Higher cost of living, and
- Not as much housing is available

COUNTRY LIVING

PROS
- More land available
- New vacation homes available
- Less people, and
- Cost of living is lower

CONS
- Fewer schools to choose from
- Further from grocery stores and other stores
- Less people
- Not as many cultural events, and
- Longer commute to amenities

SUBURBAN LIVING

PROS
- Close to city and country
- More land
- Cost of living is less expensive than city living
- Close to cultural events, and
- Community feeling

CONS
- More people in a smaller area
- Fewer schools to choose from, and
- Longer commute to amenities

BEACH LIVING

PROS
- Close to city and country
- Close to the beach or ocean
- Close to cultural events, and
- Community feeling

CONS
- Cost of living just as expensive as the city
- Potential for severe weather
- Tourist feeling

When choosing the type of environment you would like to purchase in, the following may play a role in your final decision:

- Finances
- Size of vacation home desired
- Taxes, and
- Insurance
- Homeowner association dues

You should check out all of your options. While there will always be pros and cons, you should be able to find a vacation home that will help you lead the type of lifestyle that is important to you, your family and your guests.

Grocery Shopping and Other Necessities

While vacationing in the country may seem peaceful, your guests should be prepared to do a lot more driving. The nearest grocery store or pharmacy may be thirty minutes or further. This is another factor you should consider when buying a vacation home. While small towns have centralized areas where the shops and grocery stores are located, unless your property is in town, guests will have to drive a longer distance.

Many people that vacation in the country will adjust their routines as well as their priorities. They may go to the grocery store just once, or consider grocery pickup or delivery; they will not eat at restaurants as often, and will not go to the movies or other social events as often either because of the travel distance required.

Before buying a vacation home, survey the town to see what is available. This will give you a good idea of what it would be like for your guests to vacation in an area. Spend a few days there if possible. This will save you from making a huge mistake later.

If you are planning to purchase in the city, guests will have the advantages of public transportation, but may still need a car for larger grocery trips. While the city can be convenient in many ways, parking a car is not one of them. Guests may have to pay for garage parking in many instances, which will end up increasing the expenses for their vacation. However, they will be able to get to these stores quickly and easily at any time during the day.

Other Location Considerations

Other location considerations include:

- Weather
- Road conditions
- Location of property in the neighborhood

You should also be thinking ahead in terms of the weather. If you are planning on purchasing in the country, for example, you should pay attention to possible flooding, snow, and other weather that could affect travel behaviors. If the road is a dirt road, you should ask if the county will clear the road and how often they will do so. This is another advantage of living in the city because guests could always use public transportation if they do not want to drive.

The location of the property is also important. If the property is located at the bottom of a slope, you may have flooding issues after a rainstorm. Also, as your family grows, you may need more room if you plan to use the space. You should find property with additional space if necessary. Investing in a vacation home requires a great deal of thought and planning. Even if you do not have a family, you should find a vacation home that will allow you to grow as your interests change.

Chapter 2

If you are like many people, chances are good you looked around different neighborhoods, saw a few vacation homes that were for sale, maybe visited an open house or two, and then felt stuck. What is the next step? Approach the vacation home owner? Visit a real estate agent?

Finding the right real estate agent when buying a vacation home depends on what you are looking for in a vacation home. You may have to visit several real estate agents before finding one that listens to your wants and needs. After all, you will probably be paying them a commission once you have found a vacation home, so you should be comfortable working with them during the house hunting process.

Choosing A Real Estate Agent

There are a few ways to find a reliable real estate agent. For example, you can:

- Ask friends and family
- Ask other real estate agents
- Attend a few open houses and meet real estate agents

- Find ads online or in the newspaper
- Walk into a local office, or
- Look for local real estate agents online or by paying attention to for sale signs in the area

Asking plenty of questions before looking at vacation homes may seem like a lot of work, but when you visit a real estate agent for the first time, you should think about questions that will help you get to know this person who is going to help you find your dream vacation home. The five best questions to ask are:

1. Are you a Realtor? (While all agents need to be licensed in the states they are selling properties in, not all real estate agents belong to the National Association of Realtors.) A Realtor is a trademarked term that refers to a real estate agent who is an active member of the (NAR), the largest trade association in the United States. And the Code of Ethics is what separates a Realtor from a Real Estate Agent.
2. How long have you been in the real estate business?
3. Which neighborhoods or areas are you the most familiar with?
4. How will you get paid?
5. How do you communicate?

Once you have asked these questions, you should be looking for honest and complete answers, good communication, and eye contact. These are questions that the real estate agent should have practice in answering and should not have to give you a standard 'salesperson' answer.

If you feel uncomfortable, then you are under no obligation to continue with this real estate agent. Normally, if a real estate agent does not have properties that fit what you are looking for, they will recommend you to another real estate agent in the group. This is also a good sign because it shows that the group is looking out for your interests and the interests of its employees.

You should also pay attention to:

- How well your real estate agent listens to what you are looking for
- How well they understand current real estate law
- How many other clients they seem to have
- How they speak to their co workers
- How often they communicate with you on the phone, email and/or text

In the end, you should be the judge of the real estate agent. If they know what they are talking about, can find out the information you need quickly, and are willing to take the time to listen to what you need, then you should work very well with them.

In some cases, you may be asked to sign an agreement that states you will only be working with a specific real estate agency or agent when looking for a vacation home. You are under no obligation to sign this paperwork and you should only do so if you feel very comfortable.

In most real estate markets, it's normal for an agent to ask you to sign one of these. You will have to sign it when you write your first offer, so know what you're signing. Here's a tip.... If you aren't interested in a long term commitment, consider signing a 1 day or 1 week agreement.

During your search for a real estate agent, you will find a variety of agents that will want to work with you. These include:
- Experienced agents
- New agents
- Pushy agents
- Absentee agents, and
- Hard working agents

While all real estate agents have different personalities, you should decide which ones you will want to work with when looking for your new vacation home.

Experienced Agents vs. New Agents

This is an age-old debate that should be addressed. While an experienced agent may have sold more vacation homes, and earned more commissions, new agents can be just as helpful and need to get some sales under their belt, which may prompt them to work harder for you.

While you should ask about their experience, you should take into consideration other traits such as the ability to listen and the ability to only show you vacation homes in your price range. Experienced agents and new agents have been trained in a similar fashion.

There are experienced agents out there who will drag their feet because they are over confident or they are not as interested in their jobs as they once were. Experienced agents may know more about different areas, but some of them are not as proactive as they used to be.

You should not let inexperience deter you when looking for an agent. Many times, new agents will work harder because they want to gain a reputation that they can use to build confidence in their future clients

Pushy Agents

Unfortunately, you will meet real estate agents that will want to sell you more vacation home than you need. To earn larger commissions or to sell those properties that are more difficult, many agents will try this tactic. This is where you will need to stand firm. You do not want to waste your time looking at vacation homes that are beyond your price range unless you can find a way to lower the price.

While looking at possible vacation homes is exciting, this will not last long as you will grow weary of spending all your available time looking for a vacation home. If an agent keeps showing you vacation homes that are out of your price range, then you should consider finding another agent.

Absentee Agents

Absentee real estate agents are those agents who show you a few vacation homes and then disappear for a few weeks. These agents may be overworked, may not be able to find a vacation home in your price range or neighborhood, or have higher priced commissions to find. Whatever the reasons, this is unprofessional behavior and should be rectified immediately, especially if you need to find a vacation home quickly.

If an agent does not have vacation homes in your price range or area, they should recommend another agent in the group. Agencies never want to lose customers. If your agent does not do this, find a new one.

Even agents that are overworked have time to make a quick phone call. If you do not hear from your agent in a week after your last meeting, find another agent.

Hard Working Agents

These are the best agents to find when you are buying your vacation home. If you find an agent like this one, do not lose them. These are the agents that will follow every lead, pass your wants, and needs to another agent, and try their best to find you a vacation home. You should expect to see a handful of vacation homes when working with an agent like this one.

Now that you know more about what to look for in a real estate agent, you should feel a little more comfortable about working with one. They can be an invaluable source of information when you want to know more about vacation homes and other questions about the communities you are looking at.

When looking at vacation homes with your real estate agent, you should ask questions about the vacation home, the neighborhood, the city or town, and any other questions you need to know to make an informed decision. Part of your real estate agents job is to research vacation homes and neighborhoods so that they can answer questions that may come up.

Preparing to See Homes with Your Real Estate Agent

Create A List

Once you have found a real estate agent you are comfortable with, you will want to make the most of your time when house hunting. Giving your real estate agent a list of what you are looking for will help narrow the search and save everyone some time. Your list should include:
- Your price range

- Number of bedrooms you want
- Number of bathrooms
- Size of property
- Basement (finished or unfinished)
- If you want a porch, patio, or balcony
- Central heat and air conditioning
- Garage
- Neighborhood, and
- Any other amenities you would like

Giving your real estate agent a list of your preferences will allow them to spend more time researching vacation homes that fit the criteria. You should list these amenities from greatest to least important because no vacation home is perfect and you will not get everything you want or need. Let your agent know that you are flexible, but that you really want to concentrate on certain items when looking for a vacation home.

Viewing Homes

When looking at vacation homes with your agent, be sure to ask any questions you may have. While these questions may seem small, they may be important to your happiness. Common questions people ask their agents are:
- How old is the vacation home?
- How many owners has the vacation

home had?
- What kinds of renovations have been done to the vacation home?
- How old is the plumbing?
- How low are the sellers willing to go?
- How old is the carpeting and flooring?
- How old are the windows?

While your agent may answer some of these questions before you ask them, you should ask any questions that may influence your decision to buy a vacation home. If you do not want to put too much work into fixing up the vacation home, you may want to buy a vacation home that is ten years old or less.

If your agent does not know all the answers to your questions, they should be able to find out and will give you an answer within a day or two.

Taking Pictures

One of the best ways to remember the vacation homes you have seen is to bring your camera and take pictures. Get permission from the agent first before taking pictures of another person's vacation home.

Many times, after looking at a few houses,

you will forget how big the kitchen in vacation home number two was in comparison to vacation home number five. Having pictures will give you a better idea of the square footage and how much room you should work with.

Narrowing Down Your Choices

After a few weeks of viewing vacation homes that fit what you are looking for, you should be close to finding a vacation home that you will want to make a bid on. If you have other vacation homes you would like to see or you have changed your mind as to what you are looking for, you should tell your agent so that they can look for other vacation homes.

Many times, if a person likes the neighborhood but not the vacation home they were shown, they will want to see other vacation homes in the area that are for sale. You should ask to see all the vacation homes available in your price range.

If you are still not finding a vacation home that you like, you may need to change the area you are looking at. While this can seem disappointing, your real estate agent will be happy to show you vacation homes in different areas. Sometimes if you compare vacation homes to one another, you will find redeeming qualities in a vacation home you have already seen.

Once you have found a vacation home that you like, you should make an offer. Contact your agent as soon as you can so that they can draw up the paperwork, contact the buyer's agent, and make an offer before another person does. Make an offer as soon as you can to avoid a bidding war.

Bidding can be long and drawn out in some cases. If you do not have the time to wait out a bid or if you cannot bid any higher, then you may begin looking for another vacation home to purchase. While this can set you back, you should try to stay positive and find a vacation home that is right for you.

Your agent should be there to guide you along during this time. Ask all the questions you need before making an offer on a vacation home.

Information Real Estate Agents Should Tell You
There is plenty of information that real estate agents can tell you about the

vacation homes you will be viewing. Things they should tell you include:
- The price of the vacation home
- The age of the vacation home
- Any renovations that have been done
- Any other Issues with the vacation home
- Property taxes
- Community dues
- Schools, and
- The median age of those who live in the neighborhood

Usually, if a real estate agent does not have the information you request on hand, they will be able to look it up once they are back at their office. You should be able to find out all the information you need to know to make an informed decision about buying a vacation home. Real estate agents are required by law to give you information concerning repairs, damage, and the history of a vacation home. This includes any incidents that have occurred inside the vacation home such as criminal activity, fire, and other events.

You can also do a little research of your own by using the Internet, which is a wonderful tool to use when searching for a vacation home. You can research past events that have taken place in the area, the vacation home itself, or the town where you want to live. Knowing a little history may prompt you to look elsewhere or make an offer.

Other information real estate agents can tell you include:

- Homeowner price reduction (your real estate agent will talk with the seller's real estate agent once you have made an offer or want to make an offer to see how low the owners will go to sell the vacation home)
- Prices of other vacation homes in the area that are comparable to the one you are considering buying
- How quickly the owner wants or needs to sell their vacation home
- How much you should pay in property taxes each year, on average
- Other taxes in the area

Your real estate agent is a person that should be well acquainted with the areas you are looking at when buying your first vacation home. Don't be afraid to ask many questions.

Working with Seller's and Buyer's Agents

As a vacation home buyer, your real estate agent is considered the buyer's agent. While some people will forego hiring an agent at first when looking for a vacation home to save money on commission costs, they will usually end up hiring an agent to:

- Handle negotiations with sellers
- Do paperwork, and
- Survey neighborhoods

It is in your best interest to hire an agent to make buying a vacation home a much easier, and faster process.

Negotiations with Sellers

Most people who sell their vacation homes are also working with an agent. This agent is known as a seller's agent. If you choose not to hire an agent, you will be dealing with a seller's agent who is looking out for the vacation homeowner's interests, and not yours.

Sometimes, though, the seller's agent and the buyer's agent can be the same agent. This means that your agent is looking after the interests of everyone involved. This is a rare occurrence, and it is best to hire a real estate agent that can negotiate with other agents to get you the best deal on a vacation home.

Negotiating with agents can take a week or more depending on how high you are willing to go and how low the owners are willing to go. This can become a complicated game once you introduce inspectors. After an initial property inspection, if you feel there are repairs that should be made prior to the sale of the vacation home, or if you want a price reduction because of the repairs you must make, you should negotiate with the owners to settle on a fair price. Without an agent, you should do all of this work yourself.

Paperwork

When buying a vacation home, there is a lot of paperwork that must be reviewed and completed before the closing. This paperwork can include:

Peace of Mind

The essential point is that as a buyer, a buyer's agent is the best resource when it comes to finding and making an offer on a vacation home. While a seller's agent will be able to tell you the basics about a vacation home, they are working for the vacation homeowner. They will not try to get you the lowest price for the vacation home. If you enjoy negotiating, then working with seller's agents might be for you. But if you are like most people, hiring an agent to work on your side will make the entire process more enjoyable and worthwhile in the end.

Wealth of Knowledge

Your agent will be very knowledgeable about negotiating the right price for your new vacation home, they will be able to help you decide where you want to live, and they will be able to guide you in buying or walking away from any property you are not sure about. This is why it is so important to talk with your agent and ask as many questions as you can before buying a vacation home.

Confidence

If you are having doubts about purchasing the vacation home you have made an offer on, then you should tell your agent right away so that they can postpone the offer made and help you reexamine what it is you are looking for in a vacation home. Many times, the initial shock of being a vacation home owner can be overwhelming. Sometimes talking with your agent is enough to resolve your feelings. Other times, you may need to see a few more vacation homes before deciding. Your agent will be able to give you practical advice during this time.

Chapter 3

Now that you know more about finding a real estate agent, you should begin watching the housing market carefully in the weeks or months before buying your vacation home to get a feel for whether it is in your favor.

Watching the Housing Market

For the past several years, the housing market has been favoring sellers. Market values have been soaring recently, but the housing market can be very fickle. Depending on where you want to purchase, you may end up having to pay more than expected for the vacation home of your dreams.

Therefore, watching the market, surveying neighborhoods, and finding a good agent will help you in your search.

While you should not become a captive to the housing market, you should keep the following in mind before buying your vacation home:

- The past market value of the vacation home you are interested in buying
- How much vacation home your budget can get you in different neighborhoods and towns
- Neighborhood value
- How much the vacation home should increase over time, and
- Price reductions that may be available

Just because you buy a vacation home for a great deal does not mean you will make a huge profit when it is time to sell it. The housing market will continue to change and since this is your first time buying a vacation home, you may want to choose something you can pay off quickly and make a larger profit in the future.

Also, remember that any improvements you make on the vacation home will increase its overall value. Just don't spend too much money on improvements. Creating a home improvement budget and sticking with it will help you make those monthly mortgage payments and other payments that will be due.

One of the biggest mistakes that first time vacation homeowners can make is buying a vacation home for a lot less than they budgeted and then making improvements that will end up costing more money in the end. If you can find a great deal on a vacation home, use that extra money as a cushion in case you lose your job or are too ill to work. Owning a vacation home is a big responsibility. Knowing how the market is moving and spending your money wisely will help when you are creating a budget, applying for a mortgage, and deciding how much to put down on a vacation home.

Making the Most of The Housing Market

While you should be watching the housing market, there are other areas of interest you should be watching also, such as:

- National interest rates for mortgages
- Building rates in your area
- Number of foreclosures in your area, and
- Stock market and gasoline prices

National Interest Rates for Mortgages

Even though the housing market may be going your way does not mean that the interest rates you could be paying are advantageous. In the times when the housing market has taken a slump, interest rates tend to rise to retain the natural balance within the economy.

The interest rate you receive will depend on many factors, including:

- Other loans
- Current credit score
- Credit history
- Number of credit cards
- Yearly income
- Owed debts
- Current interest rates
- Type of lender
- Time of year, and
- Adjustable and fixed rate mortgage

If you see housing prices dropping, you may opt to buy a larger vacation home than you would have if the prices had been higher a year ago, while you will be saving money on that end, you may be paying more each month because of the interest rate you received.

Building Rates in Your Area

If you notice the housing market has also caused the building of new vacation homes in your area to decrease, then you may have to enter a bidding war to buy your first vacation home. When new vacation home construction goes down, this can mean one of several things:

- The area is no longer popular
- The interest in buying a new vacation home has diminished
- People can no longer afford to purchase new vacation homes
- People are opting for older vacation homes that are less expensive to heat and keep cool during the year

While that real estate slump may bring a reduction of housing prices, you should consider making a bid soon after finding the vacation home of your dreams because bidding wars will only end up costing you more money.

Number of Foreclosures in Your Area

When looking for a vacation home, you should consider looking at vacation homes that are under foreclosure. This can be for many reasons, but usually banks that hold the titles want to unload these vacation homes quickly so that they do not lose more money than necessary. Many times, auctions will be held or the vacation home will be advertised as a foreclosure in the newspaper or online.

You should check out these vacation homes because you may find exactly what you are looking for in a vacation home.

Stock Market and Gasoline Prices

Even if you do not play the stock market game or own a car, you should still pay attention to these areas because they are usually what will dictate housing prices and the cost to heat and cool the vacation home.

When the stock market is doing well many people will spend their money more freely, which will give way to higher housing prices. But when gasoline prices go up so will the price to heat and cool a vacation home, which may make vacation homebuyers reconsider buying until the prices fall again.

This could be a good time to buy a vacation home if you are willing to pay a little more each month in utility costs.

The impact society can have on the housing market can be huge, and it can also have lasting effects. Buyer's markets are created when there are more vacation homes available than buyers, while a seller's market occurs when there are more people who want to purchase homes than there are for sale. These housing markets go back and forth due to issues mentioned above.

New Construction

When you think of your first vacation home, you may be thinking of a brand-new vacation home. You may get a great deal from a builder that is developing a new housing community, or you may find a plot of land that is in an existing community. This can be a great alternative to buying an older vacation home for many reasons:

- You will have a part in designing the vacation home
- You will have new appliances and lighting fixtures
- You will have new carpeting and flooring
- You will be able to choose all the fixtures, carpeting, and flooring
- You will be able to add a porch or a patio, and
- You will be able to place the vacation home where you want it on your property

A new vacation home can be very exciting, but it can also be a lot of extra work. The first step in buying a new vacation home is to find property. You should visit builders and real estate agents who will file all the necessary paperwork, permits, and other items needed to build on the property. This can take a few weeks, so be sure to plan accordingly.

The next step is to design the vacation home. This is the fun part where you will get to personalize your vacation home to suit your needs.

Once you have been approved for a mortgage, the property has passed all the land inspections, and the vacation home has been designed, construction will begin. Depending on the time of year, you should expect to wait about three months before you can move into your new vacation home.

After construction is complete, you should complete a walk-through of the vacation home, check all the fixtures, and have the vacation home inspected before signing the final paperwork. Then the vacation home is yours.

Many people hire a lawyer during the construction phase so that all the paperwork has been filed and there are no problems during the walk through.

Buying a new vacation home is just one more option you should consider when looking for your first vacation home. Home construction can vary as there are a few ways to build a vacation home, including pre-fab vacation homes that will be built elsewhere and delivered to your property where they will be assembled. Consider all your options before deciding on a vacation home that is right for you and your budget.

Resale Market

Resale properties are not new and previously owned. This can cover a variety of situations. A resale property may be in foreclosure, off-market (more commonly referred to as "For Sale By Owner"), part of a tax sale or active on the local MLS. Knowing the options you have to acquire property can help you save out-of-pocket costs up front, provide flexibility to you as well as benefit the seller. Whether or not you use a real estate agent in the resale market below are some common questions you should ask:

- How old is the vacation home?
- How many owners has the vacation

home had?
- What kinds of renovations have been done to the vacation home?
- How old is the plumbing?
- How low are the sellers willing to go?
- How old is the carpeting and flooring?
- How old are the windows?
- Is the vacation home in foreclosure?
- Are any back taxes owed on the property?

Using the Housing Market to Your Advantage

By paying attention to current housing trends and keeping a watchful eye on the vacation homes in your area, you will be able to make an offer on a vacation home that will be accepted. While the market is continually changing, it is a useful tool for those who are on a budget, who want to find a vacation home that is large enough to suit their needs, and will be worth more when it is time to sell it.

When watching the housing market, consider the following:

- The number of vacation homes that are in your area
- The number of days the vacation

homes have been on the market
- The price of a new vacation home compared to those that are being sold by current vacation homeowners
- The price of renting vs. buying
- The number of vacation homes that are in your price range
- The highest price you can pay when buying a vacation home
- Interest rates in comparison to housing prices, and
- The time of year

Winter is a good time to buy a vacation home for several reasons:

- More people may want to sell
- It is easier to make appointments to view vacation homes
- Prices are usually lower
- People are more willing to reduce their asking price
- Income tax returns can help with a buyer's budget

There will be plenty of people who did not sell their vacation homes in the spring or summer months and who are trying to sell before the winter. Homeowners that need to sell their vacation homes before a certain time are more willing to reduce the price of their vacation homes.

While you should consider looking at a vacation home during any time of the year, you will find that many vacation homes will be lower in the winter to attract buyers.

This is also the time when interest rates are re-evaluated and many lenders are willing to give loans to those whose credit is not the best. Take advantage of when interest rates are at their lowest even if it means accepting an adjustable rate mortgage. You will have the option of locking into a fixed rate later.

Homeowners may choose to wait out the current housing market, but if they are eager to buy another vacation home or move to a new place, their wait will be short-lived. Negotiate with vacation homeowners until a fair price can be reached. This is the same practice during a seller's market as in a buyer's market. You may have to play the bidding game for a week or two, but in the end, it is the person who needs to make the transaction happen the most that will end up compromising the most.

In the End

In the end, when you are ready to buy a vacation home, you should make the decision based on what you can afford and how much money you can put down for your new vacation home. If you find a vacation home that has a huge price reduction, but you are not comfortable financially, it's best not to buy that vacation home.

Buy a vacation home when you are ready. Many times, people will buy a vacation home because it portrays a certain type of lifestyle. The downside to home ownership is that you must make your mortgage payments on time each month. Very few lenders will give you more time to come up with the money. If you miss even one payment, your vacation home could be foreclosed upon. You will lose your investment and your credit score will suffer severely.

If you can afford to make the move and invest in your first vacation home, you should not wait too long before making an offer. The housing market can change quickly and with competition out there, you may end up losing more money if you don't make an offer after seeing a vacation home that you like.

Chapter 4

A home inspection will give you a chance to discover more about the vacation home before you purchase it. In case there are serious problems with the foundation, mold issues, or underground leaks, you will be prepared to ask for repairs, a reduced price, or walk away from the property.

The Importance of Home Inspections

Finding a vacation home does not mean that your investigative duties are over. Although most states do not have required inspections, your lender may require at the very least a pest inspection that will need to be conducted before they agree to approve your mortgage loan. If there are termites or other insects, the vacation home owners should take care of the problem before they sell the vacation home.

But what about full home inspections? Are they worth it? In most cases, the answer is yes. Although you have to pay for a home inspection, it may save you a lot of money eventually.

A thorough home inspection will include checking the following:

- Electrical systems
- Heating and cooling systems
- Foundation
- Siding
- Structural elements
- Roof
- Insulation
- Doors and windows, and
- Plumbing

If you are buying a new or used vacation home, it is best to have a home inspection before signing the final paperwork. Once the inspection report comes back, you will have the opportunity to ask the vacation homeowners for a price reduction, go ahead and buy the vacation home as is, or ask the vacation homeowners to make the necessary repairs.

You will receive a varied reaction from vacation homeowners. Many times, they will agree to lower the price a little rather than make additional repairs.

When drawing up an initial offer for the purchase of the vacation home, you should include a statement that allows you to withdraw your bid if any repairs are not taken care of or the price is not lowered due to the findings by the home inspector. If the contract does not include this, then you can still withdraw from the bid, but you may owe the agent commission fees.

Having a home inspection will give you peace of mind when you are buying a vacation home. Since you will be taking out a mortgage, it is important to know what you will be buying, and the amount of money you should invest after purchasing the vacation home. A home inspection will also help you make your final decision whether to purchase the vacation home or to keep looking for another.

How to Find a Home Inspector

There are a few places to turn to when looking for a home inspector:

- Your real estate agent
- References from friends and family
- The phone book, and
- Contractors

Ask around and see if you can get references of other vacation homeowners that will give you a good report. Many home inspectors work freelance and only work certain days during the week. They are trained in home inspection and many are retired contractors, builders, electricians, and plumbers who know what they are looking for.

When you find a few home inspectors, give them a call, and ask the following questions:

- How long have you been inspecting vacation homes?
- How much do you charge per hour or per inspection?
- What do you look for when inspecting a vacation home?
- What types of reports should I expect?
- What days during the week are you available?
- Do you offer septic system inspections?
- What type of licensing do you have?

A thorough home inspection should take an inspector about three hours to complete. This will give you an idea of how much the inspection will cost.

Once you have asked these questions, find out if your lender has specific inspections that the vacation home must pass before you will receive a home loan. If the inspector can complete these inspections along with the home inspection, then it is worth the time and the money to have the inspector complete all inspections on the same day. The next step after choosing an inspector and finding out which inspections will be needed by your lender is to arrange a time for the inspector to perform the inspection.

Coordinate with your real estate agent whether or not you would like to be present. Many times, the reports will be enough to give you a clear idea of what needs to be done. I recommend that you be present. This is a great opportunity to ask questions while the inspection is being conducted. After the inspection is complete and the reports have been completed, it is up to the homeowners to either make the repairs necessary or lower their asking price.

If the repairs are minor and will not require too much money to repair, they will usually agree to make the repairs. If you would like to absorb the costs of the repairs, then you can offer to do so. You should receive this decision in writing so that there is no confusion during the final walk through before the closing. At the closing, you should have all your paperwork, including the home inspection reports with you in case there is a discrepancy.

What to Expect from A Home Inspection

A home inspection can unearth many problems you did not notice during your visits to the vacation home. Typical findings include:

- Crumbling foundation
- Structural damage to floors, walls, and ceilings
- Water damage inside and outside the walls
- Termite damage
- Porch railings or posts in poor condition
- Heating and cooling systems need to be cleaned or do not work properly
- Roof needs repair
- Sinkholes
- Broken or leaking pipes
- Electrical wiring not functioning or broken
- Broken water fixtures or light fixtures
- Windows that do not open
- Uneven doorways
- Improper insulation
- Mold
- Radon
- Water contamination
- Septic tank issues, or
- Hazardous chemicals

Most vacation homes will only experience a

few minor issues, but some older vacation homes may have more problems than they are worth. The damage to the vacation home could cost you thousands of dollars if you are unaware of the damage prior to purchasing the vacation home. While disclosure of some problems is mandatory, many vacation homeowners do not even know that some of these problems exist until they try to sell their vacation home.

On the day of the inspection, you should expect to hear about some problems. You should be given a detailed report of the findings that will outline drastic problems and those that can be fixed easily.

Some lenders will not approve the home loan until the problems are fixed and another inspection is conducted.

Specific Places That Should Be Inspected

When interviewing home inspectors, make sure to ask whether the following areas are inspected:

- Chimney and fireplace
- Attic and basement
- Crawl space
- Swimming pools, and

- Smoke detectors and appliances

These are important areas that can be very costly to repair once you have purchased the vacation home. Many vacation homeowners are willing to replace a chimney cap or remove mold from the basement. You should make sure that these areas are inspected prior to the closing. You should also inspect these areas during the final walkthrough.

Chimney and Fireplace

Inspectors should be looking for:

- Missing, broken, or intact chimney caps
- Mortar between brick chimneys is intact
- Metal chimneys are not bent or contain holes and have all screws in place
- Creosote – this is buildup caused from wood burning fireplaces, and is flammable if not removed

Attic, Basement, And Crawl Spaces

Home inspectors should be on the lookout for the following:

- Mold
- Fire damage
- Rotting beams
- Insulation
- Damage from water, and
- Damage from animals and pests

Swimming Pools

When looking at the swimming pool, the inspector should look at the following:

- Swimming pool plumbing and pool shell

Smoke Detectors and Appliances

- Make sure they work
- No leaks
- Check for broken hoses or connections
- Broken door handles
- Inadequate wiring

Termite Inspection

A termite inspection is a separate inspection that will give you an idea of structural damage to the home that has been caused by termites and other pests. Most lenders require this inspection before they will guarantee you the money to purchase the home.

Termite inspections are not covered under the standard fee of a home inspection, so you may have to pay for the inspection unless the homeowners are willing to do so.

The inspection should take about an hour and will entail the inspector looking underneath siding, in basements, attics, and on the foundation of the home to see if there are termites present or if there are other insects such as ants, or fungus that are destroying the wood. The inspector will also conduct an inspection inside the home as well. Since termites can live in different weather conditions, you should have the inspection done even if you live in an area that has lower temperatures than other regions.

Termites can be removed using an insecticide that is specially designed to kill termites and their eggs, but the damage left behind can be immense. If the home has been infested for a long time, then it may be beyond repair.

You will then have to discuss a reduction in price, repairs being made to the property, or walking away altogether.

How Homeowners Will React

How the vacation homeowner will react to the results of the home inspection could determine whether you continue pursuing the vacation home or whether you let it go and find another one.

Homeowners have their own agenda when it comes to selling their vacation home. These include:

- Buying another vacation home
- Moving to another state
- Using the money to pay for family medical emergencies
- Retirement, or
- Making money on an investment property

This means that there are varying degrees as to what they are willing to pay for and what they are not willing to pay for. If the vacation homeowner is not in a rush to sell, then they may contest the findings and refuse to repair certain items. If they need to make as much money as possible, they may agree to lower the price a little or make repairs that cost the least on the list.

You should make some tough decisions at

this point. If the repairs that will be needed on the vacation home are required by your lender, you can:

- Try to find another lender
- Try to get the homeowners to pay for the repairs
- Pay for the repairs yourself, or
- Walk away from the vacation home

Whichever decision you make, you should live with the consequences.

Homeowners know they are taking risks when selling older vacation homes. But what about new vacation homes? If your new vacation home does not pass inspection, it is up to the builder to make the necessary repairs. You should make sure this is included in the contract before signing it.

If you are buying a vacation home that homeowners have already moved out of, you may be able to get the repairs paid for without having to be too pushy. If the homeowners are paying another mortgage, they are eager to sell and may opt to pay for the repairs upfront or give you a price reduction. This will depend on the circumstances. There is always a certain amount of luck that goes into buying a vacation home.

Ways A Home Inspection Can Lower the Final Price

Even though you should spend money upfront for a home inspection, you may save more money than you anticipated once the results come back. This is especially true for older vacation homes or new vacation homes that were not built using the right materials or per safety codes.

There are a few ways you will be able to negotiate a lower price on the vacation home before signing the final contracts.

Ask homeowners to make repairs

This is the best way to save money on your new home. While you will not see a reduction in the final price of the home, you will not have to make as many repairs down the road. Also, you will not have to worry about the repairs once you have moved into the home.

While all homeowners are different, you should be aware that many do not want to make repairs unless the home absolutely cannot be sold in the condition it is in because it will endanger the new owners. Even minor repairs may pose a problem for homeowners. You should be firm, but friendly when negotiating this part of the contract. If you do not want to make these repairs and you strongly feel that the homeowner should make the repairs, you can still walk away from the home and find another.

You should give homeowners a week to think about making the repairs. Most homeowners will make their decision quickly because they want the sale to go through.

Ask homeowners for a price reduction

If the homeowners do not want to spend money on the repairs that you have requested, they may agree to drop the final price of the home. While the price reduction will not be too drastic, any reduction is a good one since you should make the repairs yourself down the road.

If the homeowners suggest a reduction in the final price, you should consider the offer and find out how much the repairs will cost you. If it seems like a fair deal, then take it. If not, you can always ask for a larger reduction. Most buyers and sellers eventually agree on a price that will suit both parties.

Ask homeowners to pay for all closing costs

Another way to save money without relying on the homeowners to pay for the repairs is if they agree to pay the closing costs on both sides. This will free up some of your money so that you can make the repairs yourself.

You may have to have a separate contract drawn up that will explain what the homeowners are responsible for paying, and what you are responsible for paying. This will make buying the home much easier.

Any agreements that you make with the homeowners should be made in writing. Verbal agreements do not stand up in court, and are not common practice among real estate lawyers and agents when they are closing a deal. Your agent should make this clear to you at the beginning of the home buying process.

Do not be discouraged if there seems to be a lot of paperwork. This is necessary and the usual standard practice for those who want to protect themselves from wrongdoing and lawsuits later.

The Final Walkthrough

On the day of the closing, you should have a final walkthrough whether you are purchasing a new vacation home or an older vacation home. Final walkthroughs are a way for you to determine if there is anything else you will need to discuss, get in writing, or have changed before you sign the paperwork.

The final walkthrough will include you, the homeowners, real estate agents, and if necessary, your lawyer. Unfortunately, many buyers skip the final walkthrough in anticipation of moving into the home quickly. But you should have one more walkthrough just to be sure.

The benefits of a final walkthrough include:

- Making sure all repairs that were conceded by the homeowners have been made
- Be sure additional repairs are not

necessary
- Walls are intact
- Plumbing is intact
- Flush toilets in the home
- Garage door opener
- Test doors and windows
- All appliances that were remaining are still in the home
- Appliances are in good working condition
- Electrical systems are working by turning on all lights
- All junk is removed from the yard as per prior agreements

You will feel much better after the final walkthrough for many reasons. You will get to see first-hand the repairs that have been made, and you will be able to plan in terms of what you want to keep in the home and what you want to remove.

In some cases, you will never meet the homeowners. If they have moved before putting the house on the market, you may be dealing directly with the homeowner's lawyer. It is still a good idea to ask questions about the home before signing the final paperwork.

The Closing

The closing is your last chance to ask for changes to the contract, to bring up any concerns, and to ask the homeowners any questions you may have about the home and the property.

At the closing, you should bring:

- A notepad
- Financial notes and mortgage approval paperwork
- Signed paperwork you have received over the course of the deal
- Identification, and
- The home inspection report

At this meeting, you will be signing the paperwork that will make the vacation home yours. This is a very exciting time, but you should maintain your composure to make sure that you are getting what you are signing for. If repairs have not been made, then you have the option to wait until they are complete.

When to Walk Away

Any time after the home inspection if you begin to have doubts about purchasing the home, you should contact your real estate agent and voice your concerns. Many first-time homebuyers need reassurance that they are making the right decisions. Your real estate agent will want the sale to go through, but they know that there are other properties they can show you, so they are not really losing money if you decide to not buy the home.

There are many reasons to walk away from a home sale. These include:

- A bad report from the home inspector
- The homeowners are unwilling to pay for necessary repairs
- You find another home that suits your needs
- The price for the home is too high
- You decide you don't like the neighborhood
- Loss of your job, or
- A medical emergency

Walking away from a home is not giving up on your dream of owning a vacation home. Unfortunately, there are times in life when buying a home is not possible. If the financial strain is going to be too much, for example, then you should seriously consider finding a lower priced home or a smaller home.

If you decide to walk away from a home, you should give yourself a few weeks to recuperate before going out there and finding another home. You should contact:

- The real estate agent
- The lender, or
- The builder

Let them know of your decision and that you will be in touch when the time is right. Many times, after a bad report from a home inspector, it is just not worth spending the money on a home that will require a lot of repairs down the road. While all older homes will have some repairs, you should know the limits of what is acceptable and what will cost you too much money.

If you can get enough financing and you want to pursue the home regardless of the repairs that should be made, then go for it. Sometimes buying an older home and fixing it up can be a fun activity for everyone involved. Only you can make these crucial decisions. A home inspection will help you realize how much work and money may be involved if you decide to purchase the home.

Chapter 5

Financing your vacation or second home can be the most frustrating part of the home buying process. This is the time when you will figure out how to pay for the home. Most people should take out a mortgage loan to afford the price. Which mortgage loans are right for you? How much of a down payment will be necessary? What is escrow?

You will have many questions about financing your vacation or second home. By knowing the facts, paying attention to interest rates, and considering all your mortgage options, you will be able to choose repayment terms that will fit your current income and allow you to safely make those monthly payments.

Types of Home Loans

Deciding which home loan is the right one for you will depend on the property type, what you qualify for and what your lender is willing to give you. There are a few types of mortgage loans, including:

- Fixed rate mortgage loans
- Adjustable rate mortgage loans
- Balloon mortgages, and
- Jumbo loans

You should be familiar with these loans so that you will be able to make an informed decision when it comes to financing your vacation or second home. Each lender offers different products for financing vacation homes. You will want to investigate which loan products best fit your short and long term goals.

Fixed Rate Mortgage Loans

For first time home buyers who are on a strict budget, choosing a fixed rate mortgage may be the loan for you. Your monthly payment will never change for the life of the loan because you will lock into the interest rate given at the time the loan was processed. You can take out loans that range from ten to thirty years.

There are many advantages to taking out mortgage loans that have fixed rates. You will be able to create a monthly budget for yourself, you will never be surprised by the amount you should pay each month, and you will be able to lock into a low interest rate.

The disadvantages may not mean much to you now, but as your family or your income grows, you may want to refinance and pay less each month so that you will be able to afford renovations, vacations, and other luxuries. Since your mortgage is fixed, if interest rates drop, you will be trapped paying a higher rate. While you can refinance your mortgage, you should wait a certain amount of time, and even then, there may be complications.

For those who have limited income, who have lower credit scores, or those who want the security of paying the same amount each month, then a fixed rate mortgage is the loan for you.

Adjustable Rate Mortgage Loans

If you expect to make more money in the next few years, and want to buy a bigger home, you may be interested in an adjustable rate mortgage. The major difference between an adjustable rate mortgage and a fixed rate mortgage is that the interest rate will vary year to year in an adjustable rate mortgage.

While the interest will be capped, you will still be paying more for each year that you own the home unless interest rates drop over an extended period. Most adjustable rate mortgages cannot be raised more than 2 interest points per year, and up to 7 points for the life of the loan.

These loans are good for those who want a larger home and who expect to increase their earning each year to afford the increase. If you can take out an adjustable rate mortgage, you will be able to lock into a fixed rate that may be lower than your original rate. This is the main advantage of these loans. Most lenders will only give you two years to lock into a rate or the loan will remain adjustable for the life of the loan.

Balloons Mortgages

If you are only planning on living in your first home for a few years (usually five to seven), you should consider a balloon mortgage. These mortgages require that you pay them off in five to seven years. They have a lower interest rate that is fixed.

If after the term of the mortgage has passed and you want to remain in the home, you should refinance and choose a fixed rate or adjustable mortgage to pay off the existing mortgage, as balloon mortgages cannot be renewed.

Only consider this mortgage if you are planning to move after a certain amount of time or if you think you can pay the mortgage off in that amount of time.

Jumbo Loans

Most first time home buyers will not need to take out a jumbo loan unless they are buying a very large home. These loans are valued over $275,000 and are used to purchase land and a home. More collateral will be needed to qualify for one of these loans. The interest rates are comparable to fixed and adjustable rate mortgages, and have the same payment terms.

Now that you know about the types of mortgages that are available, you should be thinking about which lender to use. With so many lenders out there, it may be difficult to sort through all of them and find the right one. Doing a little homework will help you get the lowest interest rate possible.

Other Financing Options

Traditional financing may not be an option for you, but there are other ways to finance property.

Seller Financing

Another option you may have is to buy the property directly from the owner. This will give you a chance to see if you like living in the vacation home and will give you time to get your finances in order.

When looking at a seller financed property, you should ask the following questions:

- How old is the vacation home?
- How many times has it been rented out?
- What is the mortgage payment on the vacation home?
- What is the rent per month for the vacation home?
- How long will I have to make my decision?
- What happens if I change my mind?
- What happens if the vacation home owner changes their mind?

You should still sign the proper contracts stating that you are interested in buying the vacation home. This will protect your rights and the rights of the current vacation home owner.

Where to Find a Lender

These days there are many places to find a mortgage lender, such as:

- Your current lender
- Your local bank
- Friends and Family
- Online
- Your real estate agent

As you can see, finding a lender should not be too difficult. You may have to contact several lenders before you find a lender that will give you a loan that meets your needs. When you apply for a vacation or second home mortgage loan, the lender will check the following:

- Your credit score
- Your credit history
- Your current income
- Income of co-signer
- Status of other loans you may have
- Number of years you have been eligible to work, and
- Number of years you have had credit

There are many factors that will go into your approval or denial of a home loan. You must be patient. You should contact a few lenders to see which ones will give you the best deal. Once the offers have been received, you must make some important decisions.

You should feel free to contact your lender at any time during the home buying process with questions and concerns you may have. Other important information the lender will need before granting you a loan include:

- The home inspection report
- The termite inspection report, and
- The home appraisal

These reports are very important to a lender because they will tell the lender how much the home is worth and the types of damage that have lowered the overall value of the property. Lenders expect homeowners to remain in the home for at least five years. This will allow them to make a profit on the money they have loaned you. It is not worth it to them if you must sell the home shortly after buying it because there is too much damage and you can no longer live there.

Applying for A Vacation or Second Home Loan

When applying for a home loan, you must bring the information mentioned above to the lenders office, or if applying online, supply copies that are faxed to the lender. You will be asked additional questions that will help lenders determine if you can pay the loan back on time. These questions include:

- Rental history or length of time at current address
- Late payments on credit cards and other loans
- Active loans (such as student loans or car loans)
- Number of years at your current job
- Additional income
- Amount of the loan and number of years to pay it back
- Tax returns and bank statements
- Child support and/or alimony

Applying for a loan can take a week or more. This is because background checks, credit checks, and references must be checked first before the loan will be processed.

In the meantime, you should be concentrating on gathering your paperwork, and sorting through your papers in case you cannot find everything the lender requests.

If you do not have your previous tax returns, you can contact the IRS and request them by year. Many times, lenders will need to see returns from at least three years ago. Bank statements and bill statements from the past year should be enough to secure a loan.

If you are turned down for a home loan, you will be notified as to the reasons why. This can be devastating, but you should address the reasons you were denied. Research other lenders and apply at a later date. If you have poor credit, you may need to go through a lender that specializes in granting loans to those with poor credit. You may have to pay a higher interest rate, but at least you will be granted a loan.

Reasons for possible denial include:

- Poor credit or not enough credit
- Length of time at your job is too short
- Income level for loan requested
- Loan default
- Failure to pay rent or other bills, or
- Too much credit

Applying for a home loan can be stressful,

but if you have good credit, steady employment, and enough income, you should have little trouble qualifying for a loan.

What Not to Do When Applying for A Home Loan

There are a few things you should not do after applying for a home loan:

- Buy a new car
- Begin a new job
- Buy new furniture and other large items using your credit cards
- Apply for a credit card, or
- Default on student loans or other loans

These actions will cause your credit score to change which will give lenders an inaccurate view of your spending habits and your overall credit score. If you take a job that pays less than you noted on your home loan application, your lender may not agree to grant you the loan.

If possible, do not begin a new job until you have moved into your home. Try not to spend money on credit cards. Buy furniture and other items using cash, or wait until you have signed the final contract and are a homeowner.

I advise my clients that need to have retail therapy to shop at garage sales using cash. This way they won't get in trouble or be tempted to overspend or use a credit card.

Increase Your Chances for Approval

There are a few ways to increase your chances for loan approval that will also help you determine what you will be able to afford each month:

Pre-approval

Many experts agree that applying for a loan before you find a home and being pre-approved will help you create a budget, buy a home that is in your price range, and help lenders make their decisions faster.

Ask for only the amount you will need

One way to increase your chances for a home loan is to not ask for more than you will qualify for. This means you should look at your income level, the amount of debt you have, and the expected monthly mortgage payment. You should also factor in cost of living expenses, because your lender will. Apply for the amount you will need and nothing more.

Pay off credit cards

If you are thinking about buying a home in the next few years, you should prepare by paying off those credit cards and only using them for emergencies. Do not cancel your existing cards since this may lower your credit score. By showing you have a zero balance on your credit cards, you will be showing lenders that you know how to use credit wisely and you have been paying your cards off on time.

Always pay bills on time

This includes your electric bill, rent, student loans, and other bills that you may have to pay each month. By creating a track record that can be traced, you will be showing lenders that you are a responsible person who deserves to have a home loan.

How Home Appraisals Can Affect Your Home Loan

Unfortunately, a home appraisal can affect the status of your loan. If the home appraisal comes under the selling price of the home, most lenders will not grant the loan. This can be heartbreaking, but there are a few solutions that may work depending on the rules of the lender. The following options are available:

The Homeowner Reduces the Selling Price

Depending on the appraised value in comparison to the asking price, some homeowners will be willing to lower the price of the home if they need to sell quickly.

You should not count on this happening since many homeowners want to receive the price they are asking for. You may have no choice but to find another home.

A Higher Down Payment

Some lenders will grant you the loan if you agree to pay a larger down payment on the home and assume the financial risk. This is only an option if you can afford to pay a larger down payment. Do not risk your financial security in these cases; it is just not worth it.

Dispute the Appraisal

You can send a letter to your lender disputing the appraisal or have another appraiser determine the value of the home. You will have to pay for this second appraisal, which may or may not yield the same results. There is no guarantee that your lender will accept the second appraisal.

Find Another Lender

This is a last resort move because it will postpone the closing for another month or so and there are no guarantees that the lender will accept the appraisal.

Since home appraisals are required by most lenders, you should find out during the loan application process the policies that the lender has when dealing with appraisals. If your lender will not accept a lower selling price, you putting a larger down payment, or other solutions to a low appraisal, you should consider finding another lender just in case there are any problems down the road.

Home appraisals are based on the current value of homes in the neighborhood, homes that are comparable in size, the housing market, and the age of the home. While you can expect to hear different numbers from different appraisers, you will see that these numbers will usually not be too far off.

The only real benefit of a low home appraisal is that it will tell the homeowners to list the home for less money so that they will be able to sell it. In the meantime, you should find another home.

How Home Inspections Can Affect Your Home Loan

While a poor home inspection will usually not deter a lender from granting a home loan, you should be aware that some lenders will not grant a loan if there is termite damage or structural damage to the home due to water or age.

This will also lower the overall appraisal of the home, which could be another issue that lenders may have when deciding to approve a home loan.

If the home inspection is not favorable, ask your lender what will need to be done to rectify the problem. Many times, removing the termites and correcting the water damage is all that will be needed. Many times, homeowners will foot the bill for these types of repairs.

Additional Fees for Home Loans

You may notice that you may have to pay small fees throughout your home buying experience. It seems that every piece of paper you sign, file, or request will cost you some money. Here is a list of fees that you *may* be charged:

- Credit report fee
- Loan discount fee
- Lender's inspection fee
- Appraisal fee
- Loan origination fee
- Mortgage insurance application fee
- Assumption fee
- Hazard insurance
- Title search, and
- Title insurance

These fees can add up, so you will want to be prepared and have a little extra in savings for when these fees come up. Some of these fees can be put off until the closing, but you should be planning for them in advance.

Good Faith Estimates

Many lenders have turned to good faith estimates that are supposed to help you understand the affordability of your vacation home. Many of the above-mentioned fees may be added up and paid at the closing.

When looking for a lender, you should compare good faith estimates to see which lender is the lowest, which are the highest, and which are in the middle. All too often these estimates are too low. Some lenders will do this on purpose to get you to take out the loan. By comparing estimates, you will be able to get a better idea of which lenders are honest and which is not.

As a rule, you should expect to pay between three and five percent of your loan in closing costs. A good faith estimate will give you an idea of the final cost, but you should keep track of what everything costs and try to have extra money set aside just in case.

Escrow and Other Loans Terms

As you are going through the home loan process, you will run across a few terms that you will not understand. You should ask your lender to explain these terms so that you will fully understand the type of loan you are applying for, the lenders policies, and other information that will be important throughout the life of the loan. Here are some common terms you may encounter:

Escrow

While this term can mean different things in different situations, you will see it often when closing on a home. If you place a down payment on a home, it will be in escrow until all the paperwork has been signed. A neutral third party holds the money, such as another bank or escrow service, and will be distributed once the deal is over. You can ask your real estate agent about escrow services in your area.

Mortgage

Even though you have heard of a mortgage before, you probably thought of it as the home loan you will be paying once you move into your new home. Technically, a mortgage is a lien on your home created by your lender. If you cannot make payments on your home, the lender will have the right to sell the property to gain the money that they have lost.

Foreclosure

This is a term that refers to homes whose owners could not make payments each month. Once a lender has decided to sell the home, it will be in foreclosure. You should find out ways to work with your lender in case you miss a mortgage payment at any time. Having this knowledge in advance will make financial emergencies easier to deal with.

Mortgage Broker

A mortgage broker is a person who does not work for a bank, but rather works on commission to match homebuyers with many lenders that may not be in your area. If you have poor credit, you may want to secure a home loan through a mortgage broker because you will have a better chance than going through a bank that only has one lender to choose from – themselves.

Points

This refers to the interest rate on your loan. If you choose an adjustable rate loan, for example, your points may be capped each year so that they cannot exceed a certain number.

Down Payment

A down payment is helpful in several ways. It will lower the amount of money you will need for a home loan, it will allow lenders to see that you are responsible for paying off a mortgage, and it will move the home buying process faster. Most vacation or second home owners can qualify to put down less than 20% for a down payment.

You do not want to overextend yourself by putting a huge down payment on a home because you may not have enough money to pay your mortgage, afford new furniture, or make home repairs.

Debt to Income Ratio

This is one way that lenders will sue to determine if you can afford your monthly mortgage payments on your current income. The lender will subtract all your recurring debts to determine how much is left for a mortgage payment.

Therefore, not buying a car or spending money on your credit cards is so important when buying a home. The less debt you have will mean more available money for your mortgage payment.

Private Mortgage Insurance

If you cannot afford to put down more than 5% on a home, you may not be approved for a loan. But if you purchase private mortgage insurance, your lender may agree to give you the loan. This extra insurance will protect the lender in case you default on the loan by paying them at least 15% of the total loan value. This will cost you a little extra each month, but it may be worth it.

Credit Report

Before you apply for a home loan, you should obtain copies of your credit report so that you can check for errors; see how much money you owe on credit cards and loans, and to see what your credit score is. This is another way that lenders will determine if you will receive a loan.

There are three credit reports that you should obtain, because you will not know which one the lender will base their decisions on. While the numbers from these credit reports should not vary too much, if you see any major discrepancies, you should contact the agency and have the mistake corrected. You are entitled to one free credit report per year by contacting the IRS for more information.

Chapter 6

By this point, you should have found a real estate agent, contacted a few lenders, and seen a few homes. If you have not made up your mind on a home yet, you should take your time and keep looking. But keep in mind that if you wait too long, you may end up in a bidding war with another buyer.

Making an offer on a home is a huge step. You will be taking on the responsibility of a mortgage, repairs, lawn care, and other chores that homeowners sometimes gripe too much about. While you should be cautious, you should also make a bid on a home that you really like within a week after seeing it. This will put your mind at ease so that you can think of all the other items you should get done before the closing.

What to Do Before Making an Offer

Before you make an offer on a home, you should do the following:

- Attend open houses
- Find out more about a property
- Find out about taxes in the area, and

- Have an appraisal done before making an offer

These suggestions will help you make the most informed decision possible when it comes to buying your first home.

Attend Open Houses

Attend as many open houses as you can in homes that are in the area where you want to live. This will give you the opportunity to see what is out there, the going price of homes in the area, and give you a basis of comparison when looking at other homes.

Open houses are fun because you will be able to consider every area of the home without having to worry about the homeowners and real estate agents following you around. Many times, you may even find your new home this way.

Almost every weekend in most neighborhoods, there will be an open house. Stop by and see for yourself what the homes in the area look like and what you can get for your budget.

Find Out More About a Property

If you find a home that you might want to buy, you should find out everything you can about the property first before making an offer. Visit the county clerk's office or land records office to see how much the current homeowners paid for their land and the value of their property. This will give you an idea of how much you should offer for the home. If the home is in an area that has seen better days, then you can make an offer that is less because when you sell the property someday, you may have to lower your price as well.

Find Out More About Taxes in The Area

As a homeowner, you will be paying yearly property taxes, local taxes, school taxes, community dues, and other taxes that could drive your household spending through the roof. Before you commit to living in a certain area, make sure you understand everything you will be paying each year.

Your real estate agent should have the neighborhood information that will help you decide where you want to move. You can also visit your local tax office and see how much the current homeowners paid in taxes last year.

When you visit a lender, you should figure in your taxes as household expenses. This will be deducted from your income, which will leave you with less each month to pay your mortgage. Just because you may have found a home that is within your budget, you may not be able to afford the taxes that come with it.

Have an Appraisal Done Before Making an Offer

Most vacation or second home buyers do not have an appraisal done until requested by the lender. But you are well within your rights to ask for a home appraisal before making an offer. You will not have to share the findings with anyone until your lender asks to see the appraisal.

Even though this may stall the home buying process, you may want to have an appraisal done, especially if the home is older and in a neighborhood, that has homes that are of different values. This could save you from making a mistake later.

How to Write a Purchase Offer

This is the most important step when

making an offer to buy your vacation or second home. The purchase offer should outline everything you expect from the homeowner and what they can expect from you. You should include the following in your offer:

- price being offered
- amount of deposit on the home
- amount of money you will be putting down on the home
- mortgage terms
- Contingencies (such as appliances that will stay repairs that will need to be made, removal of items in the yard, etc.)
- when closing will take place
- specify who will pay which fees
- any reports that will be needed, and

Each of these categories should be explained in its own paragraph. You should try to be as specific as possible when writing up a purchasing offer. Each state has its own laws concerning contingency, amount of time a buyer should respond to the offer, and fees that are to be paid. Be aware of these laws before sending your offer or you may end up with a counter offer or a rejection.

Have a lawyer or your real estate agent look over the purchase offer before sending it. They may have some advice or additional categories you should add depending on the age of the home, the neighborhood, and the laws that exist. If you make an offer that is reasonable, well written, and hard to break, then you will be on your way to buying a home.

Making an Offer

After completing your research, you will be ready to make an offer on your vacation or second home. You should visit your real estate agent to sign a formal agreement that will outline your offer and for how long you will be making this offer. Most agreements will give sellers three days to a week to consider the offer.

In this time, the offer may be accepted, rejected, or a counter offer will be made. You should decide what you will want to do next if the offer is rejected or another offer is made. If the offer is accepted, then you should contact your lender, a home inspector, and plan for your move.

Most homes will go to closing within 30-45 days after an offer has been accepted. This may seem like a long time, but it is not. You will have plenty to do in the meantime.

Low or High Offers

Hopefully, by researching the neighborhood, the property, and the value of the home, you will be able to come as close to the seller's price as possible. Sometimes, though, this is not possible. There may be circumstances that may prohibit you from making an offer that is close to the selling price.

Low Offers

Low offers are usually the result of the selling price being too high, ignorance of the buyer, or the buyer not having enough money to pay that asking price. Whatever the reasons, you should be careful when giving a low offer to a homeowner.

If you have specific reasons for offering a lower price, they should be mentioned in the offer so that the homeowner has a better understanding of how you came to the price offered. In some cases, the seller may offer a counteroffer, which you can either accept or reject. But if the homeowner feels insulted by the lower offer, they may just reject the offer and move on to another.

High Offers

The only time you should make an offer that is higher than the asking price is if other offers have been made. While this could be the beginning of a bidding war, if you offer just a little more than the highest bid, you may win. You should only do this if the property is worth it and you will be living in it for a long time.

If you make an offer that is high, then you will not leave any room for negotiation. Depending on the homeowner's circumstances, they may have been willing to go a little lower to sell the home. But since you made an offer that was higher than the asking price, you will end up paying more than you should have.

Many times, vacation or second home owners make the mistake of wanting a home so badly that they are willing to pay a few thousand more than the home is worth. This is money that could be used for a down payment.

Making the Right Offer

The closer you can come to the asking price, the better off you will be. Once the home inspection is complete, the homeowners may have to come down in price anyway because of the repairs they should make.

Making the right decisions when buying a home are not always made quickly. You should play by the rules and just see what happens. If you get into a bidding war and cannot bid any higher, then it is best to let the home go and find another. You should not be a slave to your first home by buying one that is over your budget. There are many homes available if you keep looking.

How to Handle a Counter Offer and Offer Rejection

Sometimes, if you give homeowners an offer that is lower than their asking price, they may offer a counter offer. This is usually an offer that is more than your offer, but a little less than the asking price.

Counter Offer

Depending on where you live, the laws pertaining to counter offers will vary. Typically, the number of counter offers is limitless, but no counter offer can be the same. While counter offers are usually concerning money, these offers may also contain the following:

- Ownership of appliances
- Repairs
- Time frames for closing, and
- Time frames for counter offers

Buyers and sellers may only have hours to accept, reject, or offer another counter offer after receiving one. This can be a very stressful process, especially if you are dealing with a seller that has other offers on the table. While most homeowners will reject an offer if it is too low or they have received another, some will try to get the most they can from the sale which can include the smallest items in the home.

If you are determined to buy a home, but still want a lower price after the buyer has reacted with a counter offer, you can try to find a price that will suit everyone's needs. If you are making a counter offer that does not make that much of a difference, you should weigh the odds that another offer has been made, the homeowner will reject your offer, and that time is ticking for everyone.

Try your best to accept the counter offer before making one of your own. Is it worth losing your dream vacation home over one or two thousand dollars?

Dealing with Rejection

The hardest part about an offer rejection is that the homeowner does not have to answer your offer. If you do not hear from the homeowner within a week, it is safe to assume they are not interested in your bid. While this can be frustrating, you should move on. Begin your house hunting again and try to stay positive.

If the homeowner gives you a response in the form of a rejection, they may site the reason in the paperwork. If your offer was too low, they had another offer, decided not to sell, or want to wait for a higher offer, at least you can move on without wondering why your bid was rejected.

Considering Items in The Home

When you are writing your purchase offer, you should consider the items that you would like to keep and items you would like to have removed from the home. These items can include:

- Certain appliances (such as the washer and dryer)
- Lighting fixtures
- Storage fixtures
- Single air conditioning units that fit into windows
- Hardware from windows and doors, or
- Pools

You should put these items in writing so that you will get them with the home. Some homeowners may try taking certain items with them either because they didn't know that you wanted them or because they were not supposed to be sold with the home to begin with. Be sure to obtain a list of items the homeowner is selling with the home so that you can compare it to your list.

This can also work in reverse. If there are items that you would like removed from the home or the property before you move in, you should specify these in the offer. These items can include:

- Old patio furniture
- Mechanical equipment
- Old appliances, and
- Light fixtures

By putting these items in writing, you will be helping to move the buying process along. While the homeowners may not agree with everything that you may want to keep, it will be up to them if they want to continue the process. Having everything in writing will leave people with no surprises during the closing.

Understanding the Seller

One of the key elements of making a solid offer is understanding the seller. Your real estate agent will be able to tell you a little about the seller that may help when trying to come up with a fair offer.

When deciding on an offer for the vacation home, you should try to find out the following about the seller:

- How eager are they to sell their vacation home?
- How long have they lived in the vacation home?
- How many offers have they received?
- How many have they turned down?
- Have they lowered their asking price?
- Are they relocating to another area?
- Do they need to sell their vacation home quickly?

- Are they waiting for their asking price?

These questions, although you may not know the answer to some of them, will help you make an offer that will be looked at by homeowners and taken seriously. Sometimes when a homeowner needs to leave the area in a certain amount of time they will lower their asking price. This could be an advantage for you, but if the homeowners have already lowered the price, they may not want to lower it any further.

Make a reasonable offer and see what happens. Depending on the circumstances, it may be accepted.

What to Do in A Buyer's Market

In a buyer's market, you will have more choices when it comes to the types of homes you can purchase. Depending on how long the market favors the buyer, you will also have the luxury of taking your time because bidding wars are much less. When buying your vacation or second home, you should check out all your options. That home you couldn't afford a few years ago, may be in your price range today.

When looking for a home in a buyer's market, you should do the following:

- Stay current with the listings in your area
- Sign up for free email listings and newsletters
- Check out homes that have recently been reduced
- When making an offer, ask for closing fees to be paid for by the seller
- See if there are other offers, such as appliances that come with the home
- Ask for certain allowances (carpeting, roofing, siding, etc.)
- Do not be afraid to offer a lower price, and
- Ask for a shorter response time

In a buyer's market, homeowners may offer these options to you as incentive to buy their homes. They may also offer warranties on appliances that you should take advantage of.

There are dangers that you should consider when buying in a buyer's market, however.

- If you are not planning on holding on to the home for more than three years, you may want to wait until the market changes or plan to keep the home longer. Many times, market trends can last for a few years. If you need to sell after a year or so, you may have difficulty finding a buyer and you may have to sell the home for less than what you paid for it.

- While most vacation homeowners keep their homes for at least two years to save money in taxes, marketing trends have been known to last longer. You should be prepared for this when buying your vacation or second home.

- Make sure a thorough home inspection has been completed before purchasing the home. Buyers have a responsibility to perform due diligence so costly repairs are not discovered after the fact.

Even though you cannot predict how the market will change, you should consider a home that you can afford, that you will want to live in for a long time, and one that can be improved upon while you own it.

What to Do in A Seller's Market

In a seller's market, you should play the game slightly different than you would in a buyer's market. In this type of market, there are many buyers who will want to buy homes that are attractive and priced within their budget. Homeowners will have their pick of offers to choose from so your offer should stand out in more than just price.

When looking for a home in a seller's market, you should:

- Make an offer that is close to the asking price or slightly over
- Send a pre-qualification letter from your lender with the offer
- Choose a closing date that is sooner rather than later
- Do not ask for too many contingencies
- Send a personal letter
- Promise more of a down payment, and
- Use a real estate agent that gets things done quickly

In a seller's market, you may also want to think about the dangers of buying a home. If you make an offer that is too high and you find out later that the mortgage payments will be a struggle, you may have to sell. Depending on changes in the market, this may be more difficult than when you were looking for a home.

Buying your vacation or second home

during this time may also be difficult because you will not be able to put as much down, you may only qualify for a certain amount of money which may not be enough to compete during a bidding war, and you may be out bid by those who have more experience than you do.

When you decide to buy a home, you should be looking at your financial situation, the market, and the asking price for the homes you are interested in making an offer on. If you can wait a few months to see where the market is headed, then maybe this is the best way to save more money and find a home that is affordable. This is a waiting game that no one wants to play, but may be necessary, especially if this is your first time purchasing property.

Seller's markets and buyer's markets have their advantages and disadvantages, but in the end, the offer that you make will determine whether your offer will be accepted.

Chapter 7

Drawing up contracts, having the final walkthrough, and going to the closing are the last steps you should take when buying your vacation or second home. This is the time when having a real estate agent you can trust, and a little knowledge of home buying comes in handy.

But what about all those other miscellaneous fees that will come up before and during the closing? You should be aware of additional fees when you apply for a loan and when you are closing on your new home.

Contracts

Your purchase offer was the first contract you will be involved in when you want to buy a home. You should refer to this contract during the closing period to make sure that your rights are covered and that you are getting everything you pay for.

By writing a solid purchase offer that outlines what you want from the homeowners, you will be protected in case of disagreements and other issues before closing. But a purchase offer is just one of many pieces of paper you should see and sign before you can move into your home. Other contracts include:

- Contingencies
- Builder contracts
- Mortgage contracts, and
- Closing agreements

These contracts may vary in length depending on the forms being used and the information that should be included.

Contingencies

Real estate contingencies can be added onto an existing contract or can be created as a separate contract depending on what you would like to include in the purchase offer. Contingencies can include a wide range of items, including:

- Home inspections and pest inspections
- Home appraisals
- Financing
- Septic system tests
- Appliances that will stay in the home, and
- Property surveys

Contingencies can make or break a sale, so you should be sure to use the correct forms when filing contingencies and to word them correctly.

You will need to include a resolution for repairs that may need to be done before you can move into the home. If it is agreed upon in writing that the homeowners will take care of all or some repairs that may be found during a home inspection, this will save time later.

You should also include ways to get out of the deal that include loan denial, repairs that cannot be fixed, and lead, mold, or radon that is found in the home. Having a way out of the contract will save you money and time.

If you are buying a home that is for sale by owner, you should find an attorney or real estate agent that is willing to help you create a contingency list and edit it where necessary. Do not rely on the seller's agent because they are after their client's best interests and not yours.

Builder Contracts

If you are buying a new home from a

builder, you should sign a builder's contract that states you have the financial means to pay for a new home, that you have decided on a location for your new home, and that you are ready to build.

You should hire an attorney at this point to go over the contract to see if there are any problems that should be ironed out before you begin building the home.

Mortgage Contracts

To complete your home buying, you should be approved for a mortgage by a lender and you should sign a contract in which you agree to an interest rate, monthly payment schedule, rate plan, down payment, and other fees.

These contracts are standard loan contracts that will explain the consequences of not paying your mortgage. You should read this paperwork carefully before signing anything.

Closing Agreements

These are the final contracts you should sign before you get the keys to your new home.

You should read this paperwork carefully and be prepared to pay any closing costs now.

Home Warranties

If you are buying an older home, you may want to purchase a home warranty that will cover repairs that need to be made during your first year of ownership.

While a home inspection will catch any immediate repairs, no one can foresee an oven falling apart or a dryer burning out. Since you may not have a lot of extra money left over after paying for closing costs, down payment, and mortgage payments, having extra insurance will allow you to make the repairs you will need.

Most policies will cost between three-hundred and five-hundred dollars. Coverage will begin the day of your closing and will last for a year. You will have the option of renewing the policy if you would like at that time. If you need to have an appliance repaired, you may have a small co-pay at the time of the repair.

Not all policies are the same, so you should do your research to find the best deal.

Compare the types of repairs that are covered under the policies and choose the one that fits your home.

Closing

When you finally arrive at the closing, you should expect to:

- Sign contracts
- Do a final walkthrough
- Pay closing costs, and
- Get your keys

The closing can take an hour or two, but usually moves quickly because there is little left to do. At the closing, you may or may not meet the homeowners. If they are present, this is a good time to ask if there is anything about the home you will need to know.

Sign Contracts

When you sign the contracts, read them carefully to make sure that everything that has been discussed is in the contract. Ask questions that you may have now.

Final Walk Through

The final walkthrough of the home will take place before or during the closing. This is the final chance for you to see the home before it becomes yours. Make sure the items on your contingency are in place so that you can sign the contracts.

Paying Closing Costs

Typically, the buyer should pay the closing costs associated with buying a home. But in a buyer's market, you may be able to add a contingency that states the seller will be responsible for all costs. This may appeal to sellers who want to sell their home quickly.

When deciding, who should pay the closing costs, you should research laws that may be in place that dictate who pays for what. Many times, buyers and sellers will agree to split all costs including closing, home inspection, pest inspection, and home appraisal costs. You should negotiate with the sellers to see which items will be your responsibility.

Get Your Keys

After signing the contracts, you will receive the keys to your new dream vacation home. This is an exciting feeling and one that will be with you for a long time.

Conclusion

When it comes to purchasing a vacation or second home, you will find that it can take a short or long time. Know that our team practices working on plans to purchase. So if you aren't ready now, we will create a plan to get you ready. And if that takes 1 month or 1 year, that's totally cool.

You need to make sure that you are at your best so that you can make the best decision for you and your family. Buying a vacation or second home is a very big deal.

Lastly, you will want to make sure that everything goes per plan so that you can have a smooth adjustment into owning a vacation home.

I hope you enjoyed this book and look forward to connecting with you again. For more information about vacation rentals, visit me at www.vacationincome.info

Daniel Holliday

Notes

Notes

Notes

Notes

Notes

Notes

www.ingramcontent.com/pod-product-compliance
Lightning Source LLC
Chambersburg PA
CBHW042116100526
44587CB00025B/4075